JON HUGHES

PTEROSAUR!

CONTENTS

CAMBRIDGE
UNIVERSITY PRESS

UCL
Institute of Education

WHAT WAS A PTEROSAUR?

Pterosaur (Terr-oh-sawr) means 'winged lizard'.

Pterosaurs lived millions of years ago in the time of the **dinosaurs**. Pterosaurs were very strange animals. They were not dinosaurs, and their wings were not like birds' wings.

They were flying reptiles.

PTERO FACTS

What is a reptile?

Reptiles are animals like lizards or snakes.

They have **scaly** skin.

WHAT DID THEY LOOK LIKE?

Pterosaurs were the first animals with a **skeleton** to be able to fly. They had special **hollow** bones which were very light.

These pterosaurs had strong wings. They could fly a long way over the sea.

furry body

Pterosaurs had a coat of fine fur on their bodies to keep them warm.

HOW DID THEY FLY?

All pterosaurs had wings, but they had no feathers. Their wings were made of skin. It stretched from the sides of their bodies to the long fingers of their hands.

Scientists think that they ran, flapped their wings and took off. They were able to fly a very long way.

Pterosaurs flew by flapping their wings.

a pterosaur's 'finger'

WHERE DID THEY LIVE?

Pterosaurs often lived near rivers, lakes or the sea.

They laid eggs in simple nests on the ground, called **scrapes**.

Pterosaurs often lived in large groups, like seabirds do today.

Pterosaurs laid eggs. When the eggs **hatched**, pterosaurs may have looked after their babies.

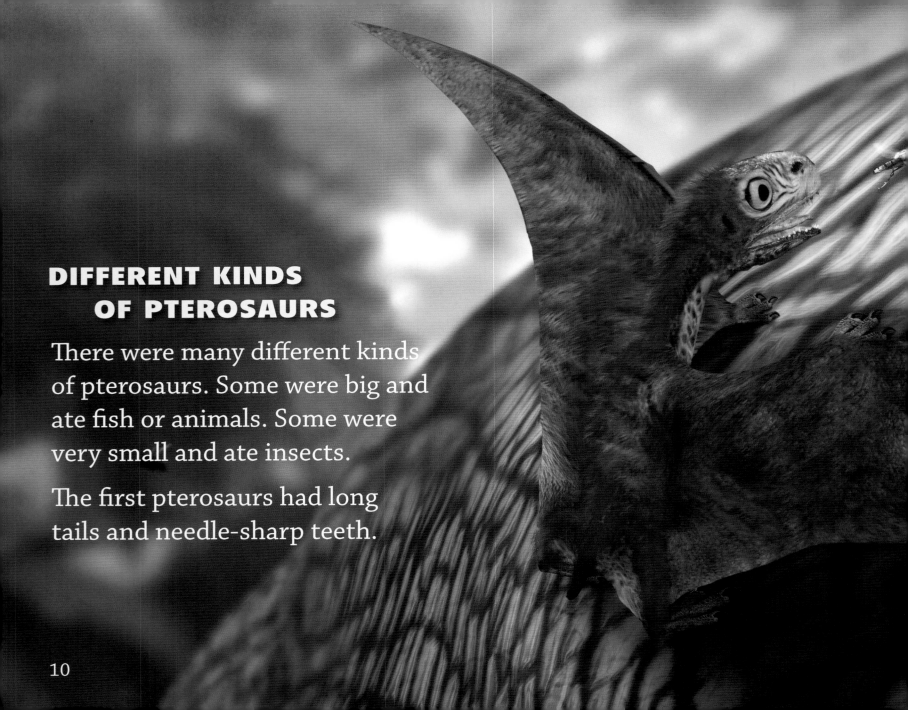

DIFFERENT KINDS OF PTEROSAURS

There were many different kinds of pterosaurs. Some were big and ate fish or animals. Some were very small and ate insects.

The first pterosaurs had long tails and needle-sharp teeth.

PTERO FACTS
This tiny pterosaur
ate small animals
as well as insects.

*This was one of the
very first pterosaurs.*

11

As time went on, some pterosaurs grew sharper **beaks**. They had no teeth at all. Their tails became shorter. Some pterosaurs had wonderful **crests** on their heads.

Pteranodon (Terr-an-oh-don) flew over the oceans looking for food. It was one of the biggest pterosaurs.

PTERO FACTS

Over millions of years, all living plants and animals change. This is called **evolution**.

Pteranodon was a kind of pterosaur.

Pteranodon
catching fish

Pteranodon
eating fish

13

The largest pterosaur was called
Quetzalcoatlus (Kwet-zal-coh-at-lus).
It was the largest flying animal of all time.
This pterosaur was so large that it hunted
dinosaurs for food.

Quetzalcoatlus was as big as a small aeroplane.

PTERO FACTS

Quetzalcoatlus came from South America.

It was named after an Aztec god.

15

HOW DO WE KNOW?

You won't see a pterosaur in the zoo today. This is because they died out millions of years ago, like the dinosaurs. But scientists today are finding out more and more about them. They are finding the remains of pterosaurs all over the world.

The remains of this pterosaur was found in Brazil.

The remains of this small pterosaur was found in England.

FOSSILS

Pterosaur remains are still here today because they became **fossils**.

PTERO FACTS

What is a fossil?

When pterosaurs died, a few were covered by sand and mud. Over millions of years, the mud turned to stone. The pterosaurs became fossils, **buried** in the stone.

Pterosaur fossils like this formed over millions of years.

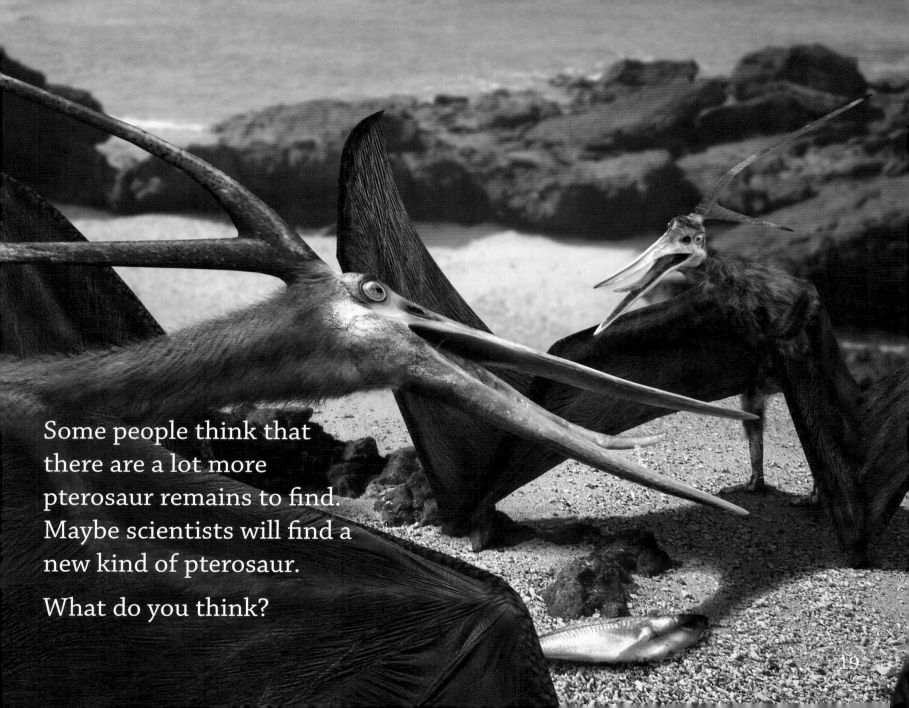

Some people think that there are a lot more pterosaur remains to find. Maybe scientists will find a new kind of pterosaur.

What do you think?

HERE ARE SOME DIFFERENT KINDS OF PTEROSAURS

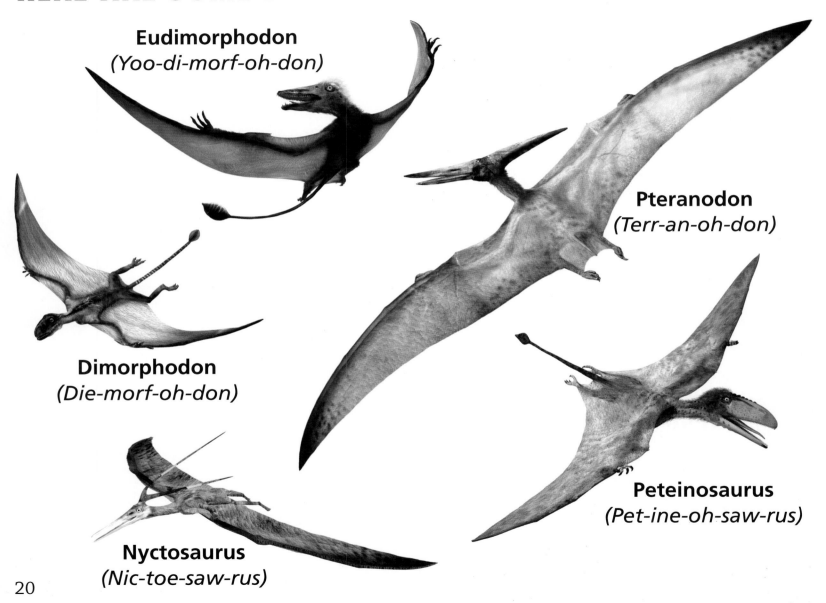

Eudimorphodon
(Yoo-di-morf-oh-don)

Pteranodon
(Terr-an-oh-don)

Dimorphodon
(Die-morf-oh-don)

Peteinosaurus
(Pet-ine-oh-saw-rus)

Nyctosaurus
(Nic-toe-saw-rus)

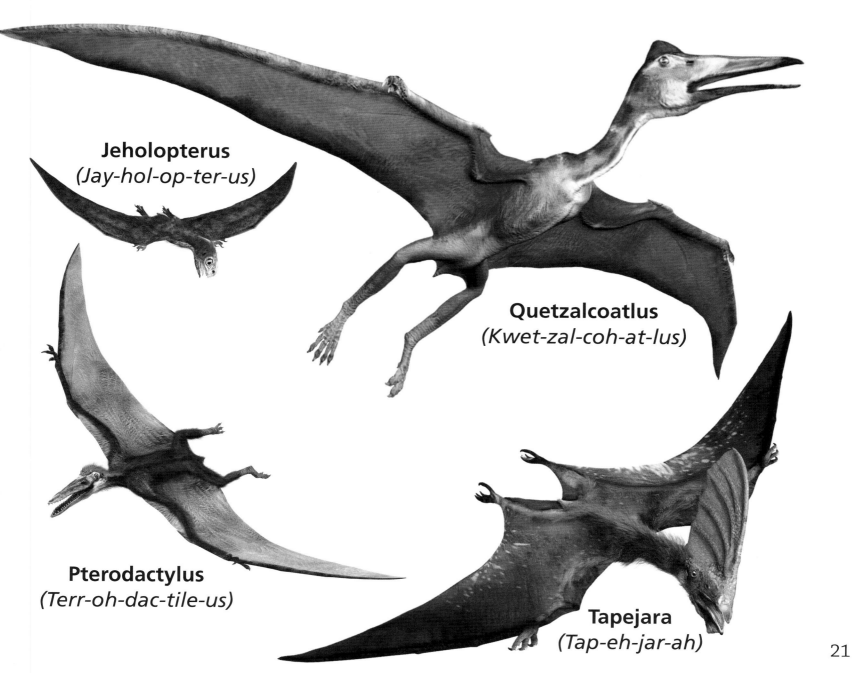

Jeholopterus
(Jay-hol-op-ter-us)

Quetzalcoatlus
(Kwet-zal-coh-at-lus)

Pterodactylus
(Terr-oh-dac-tile-us)

Tapejara
(Tap-eh-jar-ah)

21

GLOSSARY

beaks: birds use their beaks to eat with

buried: covered over

crests: bony shapes on top of animals' heads

dinosaurs: very early land reptiles

evolution: when all plants and animals change over millions of years. This is so that they can live more easily in their surroundings

fossils: remains of plants and animals which have turned to stone over many thousands of years

hatched: came out of an egg

hollow: empty

remains: something left over

scaly: covered in scales, dry

scrapes: simple ground nests, usually in soft earth

skeleton: frame, usually of bone, which supports the body of an animal

INDEX

PTEROSAUR! ● JON HUGHES

Teaching notes written by Sue Bodman and Glen Franklin

Using this book

Developing reading comprehension

This non-fiction report gives the reader the opportunity to find out about what pterosaurs were, what they looked like and how we know about them. Headings support the text by drawing information in to clear themes. Specialised vocabulary is defined in a glossary. A contents page allows the reader to search for specific information.

Grammar and sentence structure

- The past tense is used throughout.
- Sentences are complex (e.g. *'Pterosaurs often lived in large groups, like seabirds do today'*).

Word meaning and spelling

- There is opportunity to reinforce word-reading skills on unfamiliar words and technical vocabulary.
- The glossary, captions and contents can be used to monitor understanding and develop vocabulary.

Curriculum links

Science – Read other reports about dinosaurs and pterosaurs in order to compare and contrast how information is conveyed in different texts.

Mathematics – The text gives some information about size. Gather information about the dimensions of dinosaurs and order them from the smallest to the biggest. This could be extended by providing measurements for present day animals in order to begin to develop a concept of relative size.

Learning outcomes

Children can:

- solve most unfamiliar words
- pose questions, and record these in writing, prior to reading non-fiction, to find answers
- locate parts of the text that give particular information and use this information in discussion

- use language of time to express that pterosaurs lived many millions of years ago, before mankind and animals that are living now.

A guided reading lesson

Book Introduction

Give a copy of the book to each child. Have them read the title and the blurb independently.

Orientation

Say: *Let's read the title and look at the illustrations on the front and back covers.* Clarify that it is an information text. Point out the key features that indicate this is non-fiction. Draw out what the children know about pterosaurs already. Act as scribe as the children think about what they would like to find out. Jot down their questions on flipchart paper.

Preparation

Pages 2 and 3: Ask the children to read the narrative on pages 2 and 3 independently. Then discuss with them what they noticed about the sort of text, and the presentation and layout. Show how additional information in given in the label on this page. Look at how words in bold are to be found in the glossary. Practice reading unfamiliar words.

Demonstrate the use of the fact boxes (Ptero Facts), captions and labels and how they give information in different ways.

Set a purpose for reading: *Think about the questions we have asked as you read. We will be thinking about all the things we learned after we have read the book.*

Strategy check

Prompt for a strategy check by rehearsing and practising the reading strategies needed for this text.

There will be some new words for you in this book. We have looked at some of them together. Use your word-reading skills to sound out the word and blend it together. The glossary can help you if you don't know the meaning of a word.